A couple of shakes...

THE LEA & PERRINS
WORCESTERSHIRE SAUCE COOKBOOK

PAUL HARTLEY

...is all it takes

ABSOLUTE PRESS

First published in Great Britain in 2005
by **Absolute Press**
Scarborough House
29 James Street West
Bath BA1 2BT

Phone 44 (0) 1225 316013
Fax 44 (0) 1225 445836
E-mail info@absolutepress.co.uk
Website www.absolutepress.co.uk

Publisher Jon Croft
Commissioning Editor Meg Avent
Designer Matt Inwood

In association with
www.breakfastandbrunch.com.

A catalogue record of this book
is available from the British Library

The Publisher acknowledges the
financial support of the Government
of Canada through the Book
Publishing Industry Development
Program for our publishing activities.

ISBN 1 904573 29 0

Printed and bound by
Lego, Italy

CONTENTS

LEA AND PERRINS "WORCESTER

FROM THE RECIPE OF A NOBLE

– THE ABOVE CELEBRATED SAU

ITS INTRODUCTION, BEEN STEA

FAVOUR; ITS PECULIAR PIQUANC

FLAVOUR, ESTABLISH IT OF A CI

SAUCES. NOBLEMEN AND OTHE

PRONOUNCE IT TO BE "THE ONL

ENRICHING GRAVIES OR AS A ZE

GAME, COLD MEAT, &C., ESPECI

INCREASING INQUIRY IS NOW MA

KINGDOM, THE PROPRIETORS B

GROCERS AND OTHERS, MAY BE

AGENTS:– MESSRS. BARCLAY AN

MR. J. HARDING, 59. KING STRE

AND CO., 16. SOUTHAMPTON RO

AND ITALIAN WAREHOUSEMEN I

TERMS AS AT THEIR WAREHOUS

BY THE USUAL VENDORS OF SAI

1S. 6D. PINTS 2S. 6D., AND QUAR

PROPRIETORS' STAMP OVER TH

HIRE SAUCE" PREPARED

AN IN THE COUNTY.

E HAS, FROM THE TIME OF

LY PROGRESSING IN PUBLIC

, COMBINED WITH EXQUISITE

RACTER UNEQUALLED IN

S OF ACKNOWLEDGED GOUT,

GOOD SAUCE": AND FOR

T FOR FISH, CURRIES, STEAKS,

LY UNRIVALLED. AS A RAPIDLY

DE FOR IT IN ALL PARTS OF THE

G TO STATE THAT DRUGGISTS,

BE SUPPLIED BY THEIR

SONS, FARRINGDON STREET;

T, STEPNEY; MESSRS. METCALFE

; AND BY THE WHOLESALE OIL

LONDON, UPON THE SAME

AT WORCESTER. – SOLD RETAIL

ES IN HALF-PINT BOTTLES AT

S 5S.EACH, WITH THE

CORK OF EVERY BOTTLE.

From the very first advert placed by Messrs Lea and Perrins, c1840s.

THE LEA & PERRINS
WORCESTERSHIRE SAUCE
RECIPE COLLECTION

SCALLOP & BACON BROCHETTES

4 rashers rindless streaky bacon
8 large king scallops
Freshly ground black pepper
50g soft almost melted butter
1 tablespoon Lea & Perrins Worcestershire Sauce
1 lemon, half for zest and half for wedges
Few fronds of fresh dill

You will also need 8 cocktail sticks and a griddle or heavy based frying pan.

1 Cut each rasher of bacon in half, and holding one end of each rasher, run the knife blade along its length to stretch the rasher. Season each scallop with a little black pepper. Wrap each one in a length of bacon and fix in place by pushing a cocktail stick through the centre.

2 Melt the butter in the griddle pan and when sizzling add the scallop parcels. Cook for 3-4 minutes, turning once, until the bacon fat is starting to turn golden.

Then add the Worcestershire sauce, taking care it doesn't spit and make sure the parcels are well coated.

3 Cook for a further 2-3 minutes and serve hot from the pan scattered with the lemon zest, dill and a good grind of pepper. Add some wedges of lemon, hot buttered granary toast and devour.

SERVES 2

SUMMER STRAWBERRY SALAD

1 punnet of strawberries
150g baby leaf spinach
100g lambs tongue lettuce
1 teaspoon Lea & Perrins
  Worcestershire Sauce
50g caster sugar
Pinch sweet smoked paprika
60ml olive oil
50ml balsamic vinegar
1 shallot, finely sliced

1 Rinse and dry the strawberries, removing the hulls of all but 4 of them. Wash the spinach and lettuce, drain and pat dry on kitchen paper.

2 Whisk together the Worcestershire sauce, sugar, paprika, olive oil and vinegar and set aside until ready.

3 In a large bowl put the spinach, lettuce and shallots and then slice or quarter the hulled strawberries according to size. Drizzle the vinaigrette all over the leafy mixture and then gently toss the salad. Serve a plateful of salad each with the 2 leaf topped strawberries perched on top – a perfect summer salad.

SERVES 2

RIDLEY CULE PROMOTIONS

PEA & LEMMING SAUCE

**MADE FROM
MISS BETTY BOIS'
FINEST PEA HARVEST**

INGREDIENTS HERDED TOGETHER,
COAXED FROM AN EXTREMELY
HIGH LEDGE AND MATURED FOR
SIX YEARS AND THREE MONTHS

AUDACIOUS IMPOSTERS!

CHEESE & WORCESTERSHIRE MUFFINS

150g self raising flour
40g rye flour
1½ teaspoons baking powder
1 teaspoon salt
1 teaspoon English mustard
    powder
100g strong Cheddar, grated
5 tablespoons vegetable oil
120ml yogurt
100ml milk
1 free range egg
2 tablespoons Lea & Perrins
    Worcestershire Sauce

For the topping
50g strong Cheddar cheese,
    grated
Lea & Perrins Worcestershire
    sauce

1 You will need a non-stick muffin tray or a baking tray with 12 paper muffin cases. Pre-heat the oven to 210C/400F/Gas 6.

2 In a large bowl mix the flours, baking powder, salt and mustard powder together with a fork. In a separate bowl beat together the cheese, oil, yogurt, milk, egg and Worcestershire sauce. Gradually add the liquid to the dry ingredients and mix with a fork. Don't be over zealous as good muffins tend to be made with a lumpy mixture.

3 Pour the mixture equally into the muffin cases and place in the hot oven for 20 minutes. Then quickly take the muffins out of the oven, sprinkle with the topping cheese, a few dashes of Worcestershire sauce and return them to the hot oven for a further 5 minutes.

4 Allow to cool a little and then devour while still just warm.

**MAKES
12 MUFFINS**

WORCESTERSHIRE SOURCE

Worcestershire is the birthplace of Edward Elgar, the composer who will forever be associated with 'Land of Hope and Glory', the song which is sung so lustily at every Last Night of the Proms. Whilst the tune belongs to Elgar – Pomp and Circumstance March No. 1 – the actual lyrics were added by the poet A.C. Benson, and an extra note had to be added to Elgar's piece to make the lyrics fit!

ORIENTAL SLOW COOK PORK

2 litres water
2kg belly pork (in one piece
  with rind and bones in)
170ml rice wine (or dry sherry)
Small cinnamon stick
10cm chunk of fresh ginger,
  peeled and finely sliced
1 level teaspoon dried chilli
  flakes
150ml Lea & Perrins
  Worcestershire Sauce
150ml dark soy sauce
1 tablespoon redcurrant jelly
5 tablespoons balsamic
  vinegar
20 garlic cloves

For the garnish
Bunch of spring onions,
  trimmed and shredded
1 sweet red pepper, thinly
  sliced
Handful of fresh coriander
  leaves

1 In a large pan bring the water to the boil and then add the piece of pork. Bring it back up to the boil for a few minutes and remove any residue that comes to the surface. Add the rice wine, reduce to a simmer, cover and cook for 30 minutes.

2 Add all the remaining ingredients and bring back to the boil. Reduce to a simmer, cover and cook for a further 3 hours either on top of the cooker or in a very low oven at 150C/300F/ Gas 2.

3 When cooked the pork should be meltingly tender. Gently lift the pork from the pan onto a serving dish and keep warm, together with any ginger and garlic pieces. Reduce the sauce over a high heat until you have a rich, syrupy consistency. Spoon this over the piece of pork.

4 Finally strew the garnish all over the pork and serve. This is delicious with steamed pak choi, Chinese leaves or noodles.

SERVES 4-6

BLOODY MARY SORBET

1 litre tomato juice
Juice of 2 lemons
1 dessertspoon Lea & Perrins
  Worcestershire Sauce
Few drops Tabasco Sauce
1/2 teaspoon celery salt
Good grind of black pepper
1 teaspoon caster sugar
150ml vodka
2 egg whites
Few sprigs of fresh mint

1 Blitz together all the ingredients except the egg whites and mint in a liquidiser. In a separate bowl whisk up the egg whites to stiff peaks and then fold them into the tomato mixture. If you have an ice cream maker it can be used at this stage, otherwise pour the mixture into a suitable sized plastic container and place in the freezer.

2 Remove from the freezer every hour or so and give the mixture a good stir. You will need to do this 3 or 4 times during the process to achieve a light and fluffy consistency.

3 Serve in wine glasses garnished with sprigs of fresh mint as a great starter for breakfast, lunch or dinner. Also superb with a fillet of smoked trout.

SERVES 4-6

WORCESTERSHIRE SAUCED

Bartender Fernand Petiot of Harry's New York Bar in Paris claims to have invented the Bloody Mary, then a simple mix of vodka and tomato juice, sometime during the 1920s. By 1934, Petiot had moved to the King Cole Bar at the St Regis Hotel in New York. To suit New Yorker tastes, Petiot refined his recipe, adding various spices and the all-important kick of a few drops of Worcestershire Sauce. The drink is said to have got its name when one of Petiot's colleagues suggested naming it after the Bucket of Blood Club in Chicago, and a girl who frequented the joint, called Mary. The same drink less the vodka is called a Virgin Mary (or a Bloody Shame). When Tequila replaces the vodka, it's known as a Bloody Maria.

SMOKED CHICKEN CAESAR

For the salad
1 oakleaf lettuce
1 cos lettuce
1 clove garlic, finely chopped
1 teaspoon Dijon mustard
1 teaspoon Lea & Perrins
  Worcestershire Sauce
$^1/_2$ teaspoon anchovy paste
1 tablespoon freshly
  squeezed lemon juice
Freshly ground black pepper
2 tablespoons olive oil
50g Parmesan cheese
4 smoked chicken breasts

For the croûtons
2 slices good white bread,
  crusts removed
2 cloves garlic, finely diced
Good drizzle of olive oil

1 Pre-heat the oven to 200C/400F/Gas 6. Wash and dry the lettuce leaves and tear them into bite-sized pieces.

2 In a large bowl put the garlic, mustard, Worcestershire sauce, anchovy paste, lemon juice and pepper and whisk the ingredients together. Slowly add the olive oil (must be at room temperature) whisking all the time until the dressing begins to thicken.

3 Add the torn lettuce leaves and toss the whole lot together to coat the leaves. Grate the Parmesan cheese over the salad, reserving a few slivers shaven off with a potato peeler for the finishing touch. Toss the salad once more.

Pile the salad equally onto four serving plates. Cut each chicken breast into 6 or 8 diagonal slices and arrange on top of the dressed salad leaves.

4 To make the croûtons, cut the bread into 2cm cubes and scatter on a baking tray with the garlic. Drizzle with the olive oil and turn the whole lot a few times to mix. Put the baking tray in the hot oven for 4-5 minutes until crisp and golden – do keep an eye on them as they can turn quite quickly.

5 Finish the salad by topping with the crispy croûtons and reserved Parmesan shavings.

SERVES 4

HONEY GLAZED BUTTERNUT SQUASH

1 butternut squash
(about 1kg)
Salt and freshly ground black
pepper
60ml honey
25g unsalted butter, melted
2 tablespoons pine nuts,
chopped
2 tablespoons raisins,
chopped
1 tablespoon Lea & Perrins
Worcestershire Sauce

1 Pre-heat the oven
to 200C/400F/Gas 6.

2 Cut the squash into
quarters lengthways
without removing the
seeds or fibres and
season with salt and
pepper. Place on a
baking tray, cut sides up,
and bake in the hot oven
for 40 minutes, or until
soft.

3 Put the honey, butter,
nuts, raisins and
Worcestershire sauce
into a bowl and mix
together well.

4 When cooked, take the
squash out of the oven
and carefully scoop out
the seeds and fibres
from each quarter and
discard. Spoon the
honey nut mixture over
the flesh of the squash
and return it to the oven
for a further 15 minutes
until the squash is
beautifully glazed.
It's ready to serve
for lunch with some
warm brioche or as
an accompaniment to a
Moroccan lamb tagine.

SERVES 4

Right An early label
from Lea & Perrins' shop
at No. 68 Broad Street,
Worcester.

LEA & PERRINS

Chemists and Druggists

No. 68, Broad Street,

Worcester.

WELSH LAMB NOISETTES

8 lamb noisettes
1 tablespoon olive oil
200g chestnut mushrooms
4 dessertspoons redcurrant
   jelly
2 tablespoons Lea & Perrins
   Worcestershire Sauce
Juice of 1 lemon
250ml good meat stock
Salt and freshly ground black
   pepper
Good grate of nutmeg

1 Pre-heat the oven to 170C/325F/Gas 3.

2 Heat the oil in a frying pan and brown the noisettes on both sides. Remove from the pan and layer in a casserole dish together with the sliced button mushrooms.

3 Put the redcurrant jelly, Worcestershire sauce and lemon juice into a saucepan and whisk over a low heat until the jelly has dissolved. Add the stock, turn up the heat and reduce all the liquid by about one third.

4 Taste and season the sauce with salt and pepper, add the nutmeg and then pour over the noisettes and mushrooms in the casserole dish. Cover and cook in the medium oven for 1½ hours. This is a perfect dish to herald the arrival of those wonderful Jersey Royals at the start of the English summer.

SERVES 4

WORLD SUPERPOWER!

On September 29th, 1938, leaders of the four European superpowers met in Munich to sign the 'Munich Agreement'. Leaders Neville Chamberlain, Edouard Daladier and Benito Mussolini met with Adolf Hitler. The day after the paperwork was out of the way the leaders dined together and a photograph reveals that on the table in front of them rested a bottle of Lea & Perrins Worcestershire Sauce!

SARDINIAN BAKED SEAFOOD PASTA

4 shallots, chopped
2 cloves garlic, finely
   chopped
1 tablespoon olive oil
400g tinned chopped plum
   tomatoes
1 tablespoon Lea & Perrins
   Worcestershire Sauce
150ml fish stock
1 teaspoon dried Italian herbs
800g frozen seafood cocktail,
   defrosted
200g spaghetti
4 giant shell-on prawns
8-10 fresh mussels, cleaned
   (frozen Greenlip mussels can
   be used)

1 Prepare an ovenproof serving dish (ideally oval and shallow) by lining it with double layered foil and leaving a good 20cm of foil all round the outside to wrap up the whole pasta dish. Pre-heat the oven to 200C/400F/Gas 6.

2 Sauté the shallots and garlic in the olive oil until soft and then add the tinned tomatoes, Worcestershire sauce, fish stock and herbs. Cook the sauce gently for 10 minutes, remove from the heat and add in the mixed seafood.

3 Cook the spaghetti in plenty of salted water until only just al dente – no more. Drain and pour into the foil-lined dish.

4 Pour the tomato and seafood mixture over the spaghetti and lay the shell-on prawns on the top. Bed the mussels, hinge end down, into the pasta and then seal up with the foil. Bake in the oven for 15-20 minutes.

5 This dish is best served in the centre of the table, where you can then undo the foil and release the wonderful aroma. As an alternative you can prepare it in 4 individual ovenproof serving dishes so that each person can unwrap their own delicious pasta. Serve with a crispy green salad and warm ciabatta bread.

SERVES 4

SPINACH AND STILTON BAKE

250g spinach
1 tablespoon olive oil
350g button mushrooms, sliced
1 large onion, chopped
2 cloves of garlic
250ml béchamel sauce
2 teaspoons Lea & Perrins Worcestershire Sauce
Large pinch ground nutmeg
Freshly ground black pepper
50g Stilton
1 tablespoon fresh breadcrumbs
50g Cheddar, grated

1 Wash the spinach and wilt in a saucepan with a small amount of water. Drain completely.

2 Heat the olive oil in a saucepan and add the mushrooms, onion and garlic and cook until softened. Add the wilted spinach, béchamel sauce, Worcestershire sauce, nutmeg and black pepper, turn down the heat and simmer for 5 minutes.

3 Crumble in the Stilton and allow it to melt a little. Transfer to a serving dish and scatter with breadcrumbs and grated Cheddar. Place the dish under a hot grill until bubbling and golden. Serve with garlic bread and a tomato and watercress salad but also comes highly recommended with grilled pork chops.

SERVES 6

IT TAKES TIME!

The ingredients that make up a bottle of Lea & Perrins Worcestershire sauce are left to work their magic together for more than three years. During this time it goes through a pin-point accurate process of ageing, mixing, straining and maturing. The sauce begins with onions, garlic, anchovies and shallots being aged in barrels of malt vinegar. After they have matured sufficiently they are transferred to huge vats where they are mixed with tamarinds from India, red hot chillies from China and India, cloves and finally black strap molasses from the Caribbean. Then it's over to a rigorous routine of mixing, stirring and pumping which lasts for several months, before the final sauce is strained and bottled. Worth the wait though.

CINCINNATI CHILLI

2 tablespoons olive oil
2 large onions
1kg lean minced beef
1 litre good beef stock
2 tablespoons tomato purée
4 large chillies, finely chopped
2 cloves garlic, chopped
1 tablespoon Lea & Perrins
   Worcestershire Sauce
4 bay leaves
1 teaspoon ground cinnamon
1 teaspoon allspice
1 teaspoon cayenne pepper
1 teaspoon cocoa powder
Salt and freshly ground black
   pepper
245g tin red kidney beans,
   drained and rinsed

1 Heat the oil in a heavy based pan and fry the onions until just transparent. Add the beef, cook until browned and then add in the stock. Bring up to the boil and then reduce down to a simmer.

2 Add all the other ingredients, except for the kidney beans, and simmer away for 1 hour. Check the seasoning after this time and add salt and freshly ground black pepper as needed.

3 Lastly add in the kidney beans and continue simmering for a further 1 hour. Then it's red hot and ready. You can always make this the day before and re-heat when ready, as chilli always improves the next day. Serve with wedges of sourdough bread warm from the oven.

SERVES 4

SMOKY BACON & POTATO BRUNCH

2 rashers smoked back bacon
4-5 tablespoons cooked
  mashed potato
2 teaspoons chopped fresh
  parsley
1 teaspoon Lea & Perrins
  Worcestershire Sauce
Salt and freshly ground black
  pepper
1 free range egg

1 You will need an individual ovenproof serving dish, about 150mm in diameter. Pre-heat the oven to 190C/375F/Gas 5.

2 Grill the bacon rashers until just turning golden. Dice the cooked bacon into 12mm squares and mix well into the mashed potato together with half the chopped parsley. Add the Worcestershire sauce and then check the seasoning of the potato mixture, allowing for the saltiness of the bacon, adding salt and black pepper as required.

3 Using an individual ovenproof dish mould the potato mixture into a round with your hands and press down in the centre to make a well. Pop the dish into the oven for 10-15 minutes to heat through.

4 Remove from the oven and turn on the grill to medium. Crack the egg into the well in the centre (you may need to press the well down a little with the back of a spoon) and pop the dish under the grill. Cook until the egg white has set and the yolk is still runny. The top of the potato will be golden and crispy. Garnish with a sprinkle of the remaining parsley.

SERVES 1

DIJON PESTO DIP

40g fresh basil
20g fresh flatleaf parsley
100g flaked almonds
50g Parmesan, grated
3 cloves garlic, minced
3 heaped teaspoons Dijon
  mustard
2 teaspoons Lea & Perrins
  Worcestershire Sauce
100ml olive oil
Small carton of fresh soured
  cream

1 Put the basil, parsley, almonds, Parmesan and garlic into a blender and blitz. Add the mustard and Worcestershire sauce and blend until you have a smooth paste.

2 With the blender running drizzle the olive oil in a slow stream until all used.

3 Pour out into a dish and stir in the sour cream until thoroughly mixed. Chill until ready to use.

**MAKES
1 BOWL
TO SHARE**

RIDLEY CULE PROMOTIONS

**LEACH &
HERRING
SAUCE**

A BLOOD-RED SAUCE
FOR DISCERNING GOURMANDS TO
SPLASH ALL OVER THEIR CATCH.

AUDACIOUS
IMPOSTERS!

CHIANTI CALVES LIVER

4 large slices calves liver,
    about 150-200g each
Salt and freshly ground
    pepper
Flour to coat
1 tablespoon olive oil
25g butter
150g rindless back bacon, cut
    into strips
1 onion, cut in half moons
1 clove garlic, crushed
150ml Chianti (or gutsy red
    wine)
150ml beef stock
1 tablespoon Lea & Perrins
    Worcestershire Sauce
Good grate of nutmeg
4 sage leaves, roughly torn

1 Pat the liver dry with some kitchen paper, season it with salt and pepper and lightly coat in flour, shaking off any excess. Heat the oil and butter in a pan and flash fry the liver for a couple of minutes on each side. Take out the liver, cover with foil and leave aside keeping it warm.

2 Add the bacon, onion and garlic to the same pan and fry gently until soft. Then add the wine, beef stock, Worcestershire sauce, nutmeg and sage and bring the whole lot up to the boil. Simmer for 5 minutes until the sauce is rich and thick.

3 Arrange the liver on warmed serving plates and spoon over the delicious sauce. Serve with new season fresh broad beans and sauté potatoes.

SERVES 4

Right A recipe book collection from the late 1920s.

Kitchen Recipes

WITH

Lea & Perrins'
THE
ORIGINAL
WORCESTERSHIRE
Sauce

CHILLED GAZPACHO WITH CELERIAC CRISPS

2 cloves garlic, peeled and
roughly chopped
1 red pepper, deseeded and
roughly chopped
1/2 cucumber, roughly chopped
390g tin chopped tomatoes
500ml tomato juice
1 tablespoon sherry vinegar
1 dessertspoon Lea & Perrins
Worcestershire Sauce
50ml olive oil
1 teaspoon ground cumin
1 teaspoon fresh tarragon
Salt and freshly ground black
pepper
500ml still mineral water,
chilled
Few torn basil leaves
Few ice cubes

For the garnish
3 firm tomatoes, diced
1 red onion, peeled and diced
1 green pepper, deseeded
and diced
50g pitted black olives, chopped

For the crisps
1 small celeriac, peeled
Oil for deep-frying

1 Put the garlic, pepper and cucumber into a food processor and blitz to a chunky pulp. Then add the tinned tomatoes and the tomato juice and whiz once more. Pour the contents out into a large bowl.

2 Stir in the sherry vinegar, the Worcestershire sauce and then the oil and finally the cumin, tarragon, salt and pepper, stirring all the time. Chill the soup.

3 To make the crisps, cut the celeriac into 4 chunks and with a potato peeler, or fine mandolin, shave off thin slices. Deep fry in batches until you have used all the celeriac, draining the crisps each time on kitchen paper.

4 Put the chilled soup into a deep bowl and stir in the mineral water. Float the ice cubes in the soup with the torn basil leaves and ladle into individual bowls at the table together with a platter of garnishes and a basket of celeriac crisps for all to help themselves.

SERVES 6

CHICKEN SALAD LOAF

200g soft cream cheese
2 tablespoon mayonnaise
2 tablespoons lemon juice
1 tablespoon Lea & Perrins
  Worcestershire Sauce
1/2 teaspoon ground ginger
Sea salt and freshly ground
  black pepper
450g cooked chicken, diced
2 hard boiled eggs, roughly
  mashed
1 small red onion, finely diced
Handful of rocket
100g black olives finely diced
1 small sweet red pepper
  finely diced

1 Mix together the cream
cheese, mayonnaise,
lemon juice,
Worcestershire sauce
and ginger and season
with salt and pepper.

2 Next add in the chicken,
eggs and onion and form
a loaf shape with the
mixture on a piece of
clingfilm. Wrap it up and
refrigerate for 3-4 hours.

3 Remove the chilled loaf
and lay on a bed of
rocket on a suitable
serving dish. Gently
press in a mixture of the
olives and pepper all
over the surface of the
loaf. Serve with crispy
toasted rounds of French
bread, perfect for a
summer brunch party.

SERVES 4

SAUCY HABIT
Lieutenant Colonel Sir Francis Edward Young made a pioneering
visit to Tibet, arriving at the forbidden city of Lhasa on 3 August
1904. Weary after his long journey, the monks offered him a quick
refreshment. To his amazement, he saw sitting in the middle of the
refectory table, a bottle of Lea & Perrins Worcestershire Sauce.
It had got there first!

BASQUE BREAKFAST

1 tablespoon olive oil
150g smoked streaky bacon, diced
1 large onion peeled and chopped
3 red peppers, halved, de-seeded and diced
2 large tomatoes, diced
2 teaspoons Lea & Perrins Worcestershire Sauce
Handful basil leaves, torn
Salt and freshly ground black pepper
4 medium free range eggs

1 Heat the oil in a large heavy frying pan and fry the bacon for 3-4 minutes and then add the onion. Fry for a further 5 minutes adding the pepper, tomatoes and Worcestershire sauce. Continue cooking for about 15 minutes finally adding the basil, plenty of sea salt and freshly ground black pepper.

2 Make four small nests in the mixture with the back of a large spoon and crack in the eggs. Season and cook for about 5 minutes or until the egg whites are firm but the yolks still runny.

3 Put a board in the centre of the table and present breakfast straight from the pan with a warm baguette to tear and dip with.

SERVES 2-4

This jingle from a 1960s advertising campaign gets straight to the heart of why Lea & Perrins is so indispensable in the kitchen. Just two shakes will liven up most savoury dishes. And, whilst we're on the subject, here's the origin of two further shakes...

WORCESTER SEARED RIBEYES

4 tablespoons tomato sauce
2 tablespoons Lea & Perrins
  Worcestershire Sauce
2 tablespoons runny honey
Freshly ground black pepper
4 ribeye steaks

1 Mix together the sauces, honey and black pepper.

2 Lay the steaks side by side in a shallow dish and pour the sauce over them, turning the steaks to coat. Leave to marinate for 3-4 hours.

3 Lift out the steaks and chuck them on the hot barbecue. It's as easy as 1-2-3.

SERVES 4

A couple of shakes is all it takes

to quicken the heart and tickle the palate. The tickly touch of Lea & Perrins Worcestershire sauce awakens and enlivens the flavour of soups, stews, sauces — all the savoury dishes that ever came out of a cheerful kitchen.

The milkshake was invented on one exceptionally hot day in 1922, when Ivar 'Pop' Coulson, an employee at a branch of the Chicago drugstore chain, Walgreens, took an old-fashioned malted milk drink and dolloped in two scoops of ice cream. Coulson looked after the soda fountain at his store, but his creativity with the tools under his charge led to one of the most significant growth spurts in the chain's history. Coulson's milkshake came with two complimentary vanilla cookies and cost 20 cents.

The most convincing theory on how the handshake came to be our common form of greeting goes back to ancient times. An open right hand was a sign that you were not carrying a weapon. Therefore, for two men to display an open right hand meant that each could presume a certain level of trust (basically, that neither would injure the other). It's been suggested that the shaking motion ensured that weapons that might have been concealed in the sleeve would become dislodged. A variation on the handshake, where the the part of the forearm towards the elbow was grasped was also a way of checking for weaponry all the way down the sleeve. Just prey that your enemy isn't left-handed!

BOURBON APPLE MARINADE

150ml Lea & Perrins
  Worcestershire Sauce
150ml ready made apple
  sauce
500ml dry cider
100g demerara sugar
100ml bourbon
Handful of fresh sage leaves,
  coarsely chopped

1 Simply blitz together all the ingredients and keep chilled until ready to use. A superb marinade for pork or perfect for basting a roast joint of pork.

MAKES ABOUT 1 LITRE

Right The discerning gourmand of the 1930s was interested in receiving only the original Worcestershire Sauce at his table!

CREAMED LOBSTER TOASTIES

300g lobster meat
100ml hollandaise sauce
1 teaspoon Lea & Perrins
  Worcestershire Sauce
Freshly ground black pepper
4 English muffins
100g Emmental cheese,
  grated
2 tablespoons fresh white
  breadcrumbs

1 Flake the lobster meat into a bowl, add the hollandaise and Worcestershire sauce, season with black pepper and fold gently to mix.

2 Pre-heat the oven to 200C/400F/Gas 6. Split and toast the muffins and spread with a little butter. Spoon the lobster mixture equally onto the toasted muffin halves and sprinkle each with the grated cheese, followed by the breadcrumbs.

3 Put the loaded muffins onto a baking tray and cook in the top of the hot oven for 10-15 minutes or until the breadcrumbs are lightly browned and the cheese has melted. Serve with swathes of fresh peppery watercress.

SERVES 4

FIRESTARTER?

On 10 June 1886, Mount Tarawera let rip with a volcanic eruption that destroyed and engulfed the Maori village of Te Wairoa in New Zealand, a small settlement close to the shore of Lake Tarawera. Over 150 people died. It became known as the Buried Village. During excavations in the 1970s a bottle of Lea & Perrins Worcestershire Sauce was found buried in the rubble.

VENISON SAUSAGE HOT POT

1 tablespoon olive oil
450g venison sausages
225g streaky bacon, diced
1 clove garlic, crushed
250g shallots, peeled and
  sliced
250ml red wine
1 dessertspoon juniper
  berries, lightly crushed
2 sprigs fresh thyme, leaves
  only
Salt and freshly ground black
  pepper
200g field mushrooms, sliced
1 teaspoon Dijon mustard
1 tablespoon Lea & Perrins
  Worcestershire Sauce
  mixed with 1 dessertspoon
  plain flour
1 tablespoon redcurrant jelly

1 Using a heavy based casserole dish, heat the oil and very gently brown the sausages all over. Lift them out with a slotted spoon and keep aside. Next add the bacon, garlic and shallots and brown these. Return the bangers to the casserole and add the wine, juniper berries and thyme.

2 Season with salt and pepper, bring up to the boil and then turn right down to a simmer. Replace the lid and cook very gently for 30 minutes. After that add the mushrooms, Dijon mustard and Worcestershire sauce paste and blend into the juices. Cook for a further 15 minutes and finally add the redcurrant jelly – a baby whisk will help dissolve it.

3 Let everything bubble for a couple of minutes and then it is ready to rock 'n' roll with creamy mashed potato, rice or sweet potato chip wedges.

SERVES 2-3

MUSHROOM & LENTIL MEATLOAF

225g white rice
1 onion, finely chopped
1 clove garlic, finely chopped
1 green pepper, de-seeded
 and finely chopped
50g mixed dried wild
 mushrooms,
 soaked in hot water then
 finely chopped
2 tablespoons vegetable oil
1 tomato, finely chopped
200g cooked red lentils
2 tablespoons pine nuts
1 tablespoon Lea & Perrins
 Worcestershire Sauce
1 medium free range egg,
 beaten
1 tablespoon mixed dried
 herbs
1 tablespoon chopped fresh
 parsley

1 Pre-heat the oven to 180C/350F/Gas 4.

2 In a saucepan bring 450ml of water to the boil, add the rice, reduce the heat, cover and simmer for 15 minutes. Drain and leave until ready to use.

3 Whilst this is cooking sauté the onions, garlic, pepper and mushrooms in the oil until they are all softened, add the tomato and cook for a few minutes longer.

4 In a large bowl put the rice, sautéed vegetables, lentils, pine nuts, Worcestershire sauce, egg and herbs and combine all the ingredients well. Season with salt and pepper.

5 Transfer the mixture into a lightly greased loaf tin or similar shaped ovenproof dish and press it all down firmly. Cover with foil and bake in the centre of the pre-heated oven for 45 minutes. Allow to cool a little then turn out and serve.

SERVES 4

Right Be on your guard for poor imitations!

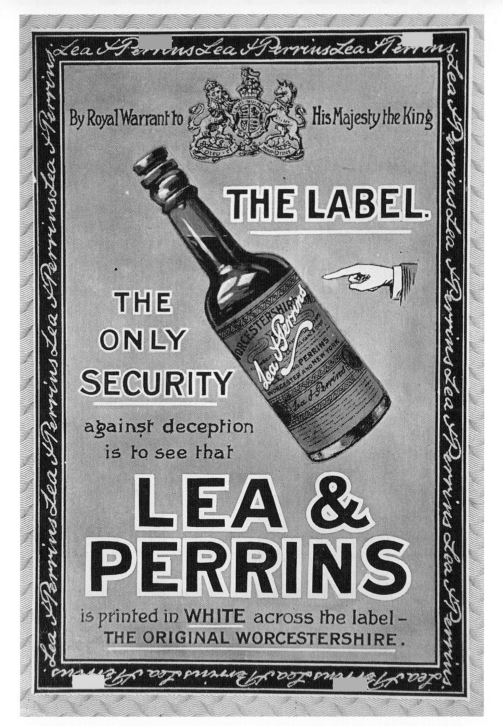

BURGUNDY BEEF

For the marinade
1 large onion, chopped
1 carrot, sliced
1 stick celery, sliced
2 bay leaves
8 peppercorns, lightly
    crushed
2 tablespoons olive oil
1 bottle Burgundy wine

1kg braising steak, cut into
    5cm cubes
1 tablespoon olive oil
Knob of butter
200g button mushrooms
150g button onions
3 tablespoons plain flour
2 tablespoons brandy
2 garlic cloves, crushed
Few sprigs fresh thyme
1 tablespoon Lea & Perrins
    Worcestershire Sauce
Salt and freshly ground black
    pepper

1 Mix together all the ingredients for the marinade in a large bowl. Add the beef and leave in the fridge overnight – or for at least 4 hours.

2 Pre-heat the oven to 180C/350F/Gas 4. Remove the beef from the marinade with a slotted spoon and pat dry with kitchen paper. Keep the marinade. Heat the oil and butter in a large frying pan and sauté the mushrooms and onions for a few minutes. Add the beef, brown it all over and then sprinkle with the flour, keeping the beef moving round the pan. Add the brandy, garlic, thyme, Worcestershire sauce and seasoning and stir well.

3 Transfer the lot to an ovenproof casserole dish and pour over the reserved marinade. You may need to add a little water to cover the meat with liquid. Put the casserole in the oven and cook for 2 hours.

4 Serve piping hot with roasted sweet potatoes.

SERVES 4

Right Always on hand as the cook's 'little something extra'.

SUBTLE SEASONING

PRICE SIXPENCE

BASIL & BLACK CHERRY SALSA

225g sweet black cherries
1 small green pepper,
   deseeded and diced
1 teaspoon lime juice
1 teaspoon Lea & Perrins
   Worcestershire Sauce
1/2 teaspoon Tabasco sauce
Salt and freshly ground black
   pepper
Zest of 1 lime
Handful of fresh basil leaves,
   torn

1 Pit and roughly chop the cherries and put them into a bowl with the green pepper.

2 Add the remaining ingredients, finishing with the torn basil and toss. Chill for one hour.

3 Great to serve with hot or cold duck, chicken, turkey or pork.

SERVES 2

SAUCY TATTOO

Rumour has it that a piece of paper bearing the inscription 'Lea & Perrins' wafted the way of a Borneo Peluan tribe settlement. No-one quite knows how it got there, but, evidence that it did was for all to see if one took a glance at the chief of the tribe's arm, where, adjacent to the tribal decorations and religious emblems imprinted there, could be seen the tattooed Lea & Perrins script lettering!

TURKEY JERKY

500g raw turkey meat, sliced into thin strips

2 tablespoons hickory smoked BBQ marinade

2 tablespoons soy sauce

2 tablespoons Lea & Perrins Worcestershire Sauce

6 dashes Tabasco sauce

2 teaspoons jerk seasoning

1 Mix all the ingredients together in a dish, cover with cling film and pop into the fridge for 24 hours, turning the mixture 2 or 3 times during the chilling.

2 With a slotted spoon lift out the turkey, place on kitchen paper and pat lightly to remove any excess liquid. Lay out the strips of turkey on a baking sheet and place in the oven at the lowest possible setting to de-hydrate the meat.

3 Leave in the oven for at least 12 hours! Probably best to do this overnight - but don't forget it in the morning. The end result, similar to the South African version called biltong, is a tough yet crisp healthy snack for all the family to enjoy.

SERVES 4-6 AS A SNACK

BREAKFAST KEBABS WITH SEVILLE ORANGE SAUCE

1 tablespoon olive oil
2 tablespoons Lea & Perrins
  Worcestershire Sauce
Juice and the rind of one
  large orange
Sea salt and freshly ground
  black pepper
450g shoulder bacon joint,
  cut into 2.5cm cubes
4 thin skinless pork sausages,
  halved
8 small onions, par boiled
12 button mushrooms

For the sauce
3 tablespoons chunky Seville
  orange marmalade
150ml water (if needed)

1 First make a marinade by mixing the oil, Worcestershire sauce, orange rind and juice, salt and pepper in a large shallow dish. Thread alternately onto each skewer the bacon, sausages, onions and mushrooms, place in the marinade and leave for at least one hour, turning occasionally.

2 Remove the kebabs from the marinade and place on a well-oiled grill grid. Brush with more of the marinade and cook on medium hot for 12-15 minutes, turning frequently.

3 While the kebabs are grilling, make the sauce by placing the remaining marinade in a saucepan and then stir in the marmalade. Bring to the boil stirring, then reduce the heat and simmer gently for two minutes, adding a little water if the sauce is too thick for drizzling. Serve the kebabs on warmed breakfast plates drenched with the marmalade sauce.

SERVES 4

WORCESTER ROASTIES

12-16 medium sized new
    potatoes
4 tablespoons olive oil
1 tablespoon Lea & Perrins
    Worcestershire Sauce
50g butter
Sea salt to sprinkle

1 Pre-heat the oven to
200C/400F/Gas 6. Put
each potato in the bowl
of a wooden spoon and
rest the spoon on your
chopping board. Cut
down through the potato
at 3mm intervals all the
way along the potato.
You do not want to slice
all the way through the
potato – the bowl of the
spoon will prevent this
happening.

2 Whisk the olive oil and
Worcestershire sauce
in a small bowl. It does
not need to perfectly
amalgamate. Heat the
butter and Worcestershire
oil until sizzling in a
baking tin on top of the
cooker and then add the
potatoes, turning them a
few times and spooning
over the oil.

3 Return all the potatoes
to cut side up, sprinkle
with a little sea salt and
roast in the oven for
45 minutes, or until the
potatoes are soft centred
and crispy on the
outside.

SERVES 4

THE ORANGE LABEL

Lea & Perrins Worcestershire Sauce is unmistakably Lea & Perrins Worcestershire Sauce.
It's become one of the most instantly recognisable store-cupboard icons in the world, which
owes much to its distinctive orange label and signature. Orange is a high-visibility colour.
The colour of the Golden Gate Bridge is International Orange. In English heraldry, orange denotes
strength, honour and generosity. Orange is also the national colour of the Netherlands.

DEVILLED KIDNEYS

8 lambs kidneys
2 teaspoons Lea & Perrins
   Worcestershire sauce
1 tablespoon tomato purée
1 tablespoon lemon juice
1 tablespoon French mustard
Pinch cayenne pepper
Sea salt and freshly ground
   black pepper
25g butter
1 tablespoon freshly chopped
   parsley to garnish

1 Remove the skin from the kidneys, cut them in half and cut away the cores. Mix together the Worcestershire sauce, tomato purée, lemon juice, mustard, cayenne pepper, salt and pepper and reserve.

2 Heat the butter in a frying pan over a moderate heat and cook the kidneys for about three minutes on each side.

3 Pour the devil sauce over the kidneys, then quickly stir so that they are evenly coated and cook for a further couple of minutes. Serve immediately with roasted tomatoes, sprinkled with chopped parsley and garnished with toasted triangles.

SERVES 4

PROBLEMS OF PRONUNCIATION

Three syllables, not four, is the aide memoire to keep in mind. Lea & Perrins Worcestershire Sauce is sold in more than 130 different countries, and, inevitably, some countries find it more difficult to wrap their tongues around the name than others. Outside of the UK, many people pronounce the word phonetically. It should be pronounced 'woos-ter-sher'. Still, Yosemite Sam got the message across, managing to land some for his steaks despite garbling his delivery as 'Warchestershershire Sauce'.

SATAY DUCK

2 boneless duck breasts
1 teaspoon finely chopped
  fresh ginger
1 tablespoon soy sauce
1 tablespoon Lea & Perrins
  Worcestershire Sauce
Finely grated zest and juice of
  2 oranges
Salt and freshly ground black
  pepper
50g unsalted peanuts
1 bird's-eye chilli, deseeded
  and finely chopped
Orange wedges

**You will also need 8 bamboo
  skewers, pre-soaked in
  water to stop them
  burning.**

1 Slice the duck breasts diagonally into 1cm thick strips. In a bowl, mix the ginger, soy sauce, Worcestershire sauce, orange zest and juice and season with pepper. Add the sliced duck, cover and refrigerate for 2 hours.

2 Heat the grill to medium hot. Thread the thin slices of duck onto the skewers and place them in the grill pan. Spoon over the marinade and grill for 3-4 minutes, or until the duck is just cooked.

3 Meanwhile, spread the nuts on a baking tray and roast in the oven for 5 minutes, until golden brown. Set aside.

4 When the duck is cooked, lift the skewers onto a heated serving dish, cover and keep hot. Put the nuts into a food processor together with the cooking juices from the duck and the chilli and blitz until smooth. Place in a small saucepan and gently reheat.

5 To present – put the skewered duck onto serving plates with the orange wedges together with little side dishes of warm peanut sauce for dipping.

SERVES 4

CHRISSIE'S RAREBIT

50g Red Leicester cheese, grated
2 tablespoons Lea & Perrins Worcestershire Sauce
Thick slice wholegrain bread
1 large free range egg
Little butter for spreading

1 Mix together the Red Leicester and the Worcestershire sauce and let it stand for a few minutes. Lightly toast the bread on both sides. Heat the grill to medium-hot.

2 While the bread is toasting, lightly poach the egg in water that has been brought to a rolling boil.

3 Spread a little butter on the toast and using a slotted spoon and kitchen paper remove and drain the poached egg from the water and place it on the toast. Top this with the cheese mixture and cook it under the hot grill until golden and bubbly. Tuck in after drinking copious amounts of cold water due to burning roof of mouth on boiling cheese!

SERVES 1

Right A First World War cartoon, showing boys from the Worcester regiment indicating to the Kaiser where they've gleaned their strength from. Many soldiers relied upon the Lea & Perrins Worcestershire Sauce to liven up their tins of bully beef.

THE OLD BOLD WORCESTERS

SPICED MEATBALLS

1kg minced steak
50g fresh breadcrumbs
1 teaspoon curry powder
Salt and freshly ground black
  pepper
2 medium free range eggs,
  beaten

For the gravy
Knob of unsalted butter
1 tablespoon olive oil
1 onion, chopped
1 clove of garlic
2 tablespoons flour
500ml good beef stock
1 tablespoon Lea & Perrins
  Worcestershire Sauce
2 tablespoons fruit chutney

1 Pre-heat the oven to 180C/350F/Gas 4. In a large bowl mix together all the meatball ingredients. When the mixture is well blended form into balls slightly larger than a golf ball.

2 Add the butter and oil to a frying pan and over a medium heat fry the meatballs for 5 minutes. Add the onion and garlic and cook for a further 4-5 minutes, or until the meatballs are nutty and golden and the onions softened.

3 Using a slotted spoon lift out the meatballs and onions and put them into a shallow ovenproof dish. Add the flour to the remaining juices in the pan, stirring all the time, and cook for a further minute. Pour in the beef stock, a little at a time,

and lastly add the Worcestershire sauce and fruit chutney.

4 Pour the gravy mixture over the meatballs and put the dish, uncovered, into the hot oven for a further 20 minutes. Serve with fluffy Basmati rice or ribbon pasta.

SERVES 4-6

Right
'The Only Good Sauce'

HUNGARIAN CABBAGE PARCELS

1 large Savoy cabbage
150g cooked white rice
1 medium onion, chopped
1 teaspoon chopped garlic
1 teaspoon oregano, roughly
    chopped
1 free range egg, beaten
1 tablespoon Lea & Perrins
    Worcestershire Sauce
 450g minced pork
Salt and freshly ground
    pepper
150g rindless streaky bacon
1 tin condensed tomato soup
Fresh soured cream

1 Pre-heat the oven to 180C/350F/Gas 4. Bring a large pan of salted water to the boil. Remove any damaged outer leaves from the cabbage and plunge the whole thing into the water to blanch. Bring the water back to the boil for 2 minutes and then drain the cabbage and refresh with cold water to keep the colour. Blanching will make it easy to separate the cabbage leaves.

2 To make the stuffing mix together in a large bowl the rice, onions, garlic, oregano, egg, Worcestershire sauce and pork. Season with salt and pepper and shape the mixture into balls using a dessert-spoonful for each.

3 Cut off the larger cabbage leaves and spread each in turn on the work surface, trimming off any larger stalks. Place a stuffing ball in the centre of each leaf, wrap up in a parcel and place in a shallow ovenproof serving dish. Continue until you have used all the stuffing mixture and pack the parcels tightly into the dish.

4 Stretch the bacon with the back of a knife, cut each rasher in half and use to criss-cross over each parcel. Pour over the tomato soup and cook in the oven for 45 minutes. Serve with good dollops of soured cream.

SERVES 4

Right
Keep it near for cooking!

BOURBON BARBECUE SAUCE

1 tablespoon shallots,
chopped
2 cloves garlic, peeled and
finely diced
1 tablespoon olive oil
½ bottle Lea & Perrins
Worcestershire Sauce
Freshly ground black pepper
4 tablespoons bourbon
100g cold unsalted butter
1 tablespoon chopped
parsley

1 Sauté the shallots and garlic in the olive oil. Add the Worcestershire sauce and simmer until the liquid is reduced by about half.

2 Season with plenty of black pepper and then add the bourbon. Ignite the liquid to burn off the alcohol and then remove from the heat.

3 Whisk in the cold butter until thoroughly blended, add the chopped parsley and it is ready to brush over your meat for barbecuing. Perfect on steaks, chops and kebabs

MAKES ABOUT 1 CUPFUL

GIVE US BEER!

In 1942, the British War Department had to invoke emergency powers and were forced to take control of Lea & Perrins' Midland Road factory. The sauce, stored in barrels and all in different stages of the maturation process, needed to be relocated. The decision was made to move the vats to nearby public houses. Mayhem ensued when the locals bearing witness to the vast inventory of barrels arriving at one of the pubs wrongly assumed that the house was taking in a delivery of beer (which was in terribly short supply at the time). The landlords protested vociferously, assuring the people that the barrels contained Worcestershire's favourite sauce, but the townsfolk would have none of it. The baying crowds were placated only when the tops from the barrels had each been removed. Upon catching whiff of the famous, pungent, non-alcoholic smell, they went back about their regular business.

CHEDDAR, CHICKEN & SPINACH PANCAKES

40g unsalted butter
40g plain flour
500ml milk
150g mature Cheddar cheese, grated
Salt and freshly ground pepper
Few shakes of sesame oil
400g baby leaf spinach, washed
1 tablespoon Lea & Perrins Worcestershire Sauce
300g cooked chicken breast, cut into strips
Handful flatleaf parsley leaves, chopped
6 ready made pancakes

1 Pre-heat the oven to 200C/400F/Gas 6.

2 First make the sauce by melting the butter in a saucepan, add the flour and stir rapidly for 1 minute. Gradually add the milk, still stirring constantly and bring to the boil to thicken. Remove from the heat and stir in three quarters of the cheese until melted. Season with salt and pepper and leave aside.

3 Heat the sesame oil in a pan (a wok is ideal) and add the spinach and Worcestershire sauce and toss until wilted.

4 Take one pancake and put one sixth of the chicken and spinach down the centre of it. Spoon over some of the cheesy sauce, roll up the pancake and place in a lightly greased ovenproof dish. Repeat with the other pancakes and then pour the remaining sauce over the 6 filled pancakes.

5 Sprinkle the rest of the grated cheese over the top of the pancakes and bake in the oven for 20-25 minutes until golden. Serve strewn with the chopped parsley and a mixed leaf salad.

MAKES 6 FILLED PANCAKES

RED ONION SOUP WITH CHEESY CROUTONS

2 tablespoons olive oil
50g unsalted butter
800g red onions, peeled and
  thinly sliced
2 cloves garlic, peeled and
  minced
1 teaspoon sugar
1 tablespoon Lea and Perrins
  Worcestershire Sauce
1 litre rich beef stock
275ml dry white wine
Good grate of nutmeg
Salt and freshly ground black
  pepper

For the croûtons
½ French stick, sliced
Butter for spreading
200g Gruyère cheese, grated

1 The soup can be made in advance and re-heated, but the croûtons need to made at the time.

2 Heat the oil and butter in a heavy based saucepan until sizzling and add the onions, garlic, sugar and Worcestershire sauce. Turn the onions in the hot oil for 5 minutes until they darken at the edges. Reduce the heat to the lowest setting and cook very gently for 30 minutes until caramelised.

3 Pour the stock into the onion pan, scraping the base with a wooden spoon to get all the caramelised onion from the base. Add the wine, nutmeg and seasoning and bring it all up to the boil. Turn the heat right down to the lowest setting again and leave to just simmer away uncovered for 1 hour.

4 Warm your soup bowls in a low oven and heat the grill to high. Toast the slices of bread lightly on both sides and spread with a little butter on one side. Pile the grated cheese on top of each slice and put under the hot grill until the cheese begins to bubble.

5 Ladle the hot soup into warm serving bowls and carefully float the cheesy croûtons on top – a sensational winter warmer.

SERVES 6

CRAB LOUISIANA

For the sauce
150ml light mayonnaise
2 tablespoons tomato
   ketchup
1 tablespoon Lea & Perrins
   Worcestershire Sauce
3 tablespoons olive oil
1 tablespoon white wine
   vinegar
1 small onion, finely chopped
2 tablespoons chopped
   flatleaf parsley
4 tablespoons crème fraîche
100g pimento stuffed olives
Salt and freshly ground
   pepper

2 ripe avocados
Lemon juice
Mixed salad leaves
450g fresh crabmeat
Sweet smoked paprika

1 Blend together all the sauce ingredients, except the olives, and season with salt and pepper. Chop the stuffed olives and add them into the mixture. Chill for 1 hour.

2 Halve and stone the avocados and then remove the skin. Lay each avocado half flat side down and cut lengthways into 6-8 long slices. Drizzle each with a little lemon juice to hold the fresh green colour. Scatter some salad leaves on each plate and transfer the avocado halves on top. Press down gently on the avocado until the slices fan out.

3 Add the crabmeat to the chilled mayo mixture and fold in gently. Pile the crab salad on top of the avocado and sprinkle a little paprika over the top. Serve with hot crusty ciabatta bread.

SERVES 4

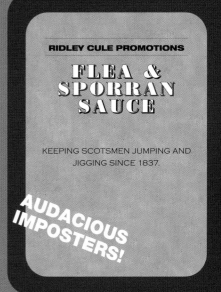

RIDLEY CULE PROMOTIONS

FLEA & SPORRAN SAUCE

KEEPING SCOTSMEN JUMPING AND
JIGGING SINCE 1837.

AUDACIOUS
IMPOSTERS!

CRISPY ROASTED FENNEL WITH PARMESAN

4 medium fennel bulbs
100g stale white bread
25g flatleaf parsley
1 clove garlic
75g freshly grated Parmesan
   cheese
1 tablespoon Lea & Perrins
   Worcestershire sauce and
   2 tablespoons olive oil,
   whisked together
Freshly ground black pepper

1 Preheat the oven to 190C/375F/Gas 5.

2 Trim the fennel bulbs removing the fronds and any tough outer leaves and cut into quarters lengthways. Cook the fennel in boiling water for about 10 minutes until just tender. Drain and put in a large bowl.

3 Turn the bread into breadcrumbs in a blender and then add the parsley leaves, garlic and Parmesan cheese and blitz for a further 20 seconds.

4 Add the oil and Worcestershire sauce mixture to the fennel and turn the whole lot gently to coat. Next add the breadcrumb mixture and keep turning until all the fennel quarters are covered. Lay them out on a baking tray, pressing the crumbs gently between the fennel leaves.

5 Bake in the oven for about 30 minutes or until the breadcrumbs have turned golden brown.

SERVES 4

Right Lea & Perrins were forced to issue a temporary label after their printers had been damaged by enemy action during the Second World War. **Far right** Back to something more familiar in 1945.

LEA & PERRINS
SAUCE

THE ORIGINAL & GENUINE
WORCESTERSHIRE SAUCE

MANUFACTURED BY

Messrs. Lea & Perrins Ltd.
WORCESTER, ENGLAND.

TEMPORARY LABEL

Messrs. Lea & Perrins are compelled to issue this label owing to the destruction of their Printer's Establishment by

THE ORIGINAL and GENUINE
LEA & PERRINS
SAUCE
WORCESTERSHIRE SAUCE

MANUFACTURED BY LEA & PERRINS LTD.
WORCESTER, ENGLAND

CAPACITY 5 FLUID OUNCES

MAXIMUM
PRICE
RETAIL 1/2

BEEF CARPACCIO

500g fillet of beef
Freshly ground black pepper
75g Pecorino cheese (or
   Parmesan)

For the marinade
5 tablespoons Lea & Perrins
   Worcestershire Sauce
5 tablespoons dark soy sauce
10 tablespoons balsamic
   vinegar
500ml olive oil
300ml dry white wine
5 garlic cloves, finely
   chopped
1 tablespoon fresh thyme
   leaves
Handful fresh basil leaves,
   roughly torn
Sea salt and freshly ground
   black pepper

1 Remove any fat from around the piece of beef and discard.

2 In a bowl, large enough to hold the beef, put all the liquid ingredients of the marinade and mix well with a whisk. Add the garlic, herbs (all but a few basil leaves for the finishing touch), plenty of black pepper and the sea salt and then immerse the beef in the marinade.

3 Cover the bowl with cling film and refrigerate for 5 days, turning the beef in the delicious juices at least once every day.

4 Remove the beef from the marinade, wrap in cling film and chill for a further few hours. It can also be wholly or partly frozen at this stage depending on how much you need to use.

5 Cut the beef into 1cm thick slices. Put a slice at a time between 2 sheets of cling film and with a rolling pin and a little pressure gently roll out each slice until you have a wafer thin piece of meat. Repeat with the remaining slices. To serve, divide the beef between your serving plates, drizzle with a few teaspoons of the marinade, scatter a few basil leaves over and finally, using a potato peeler, add shavings of Pecorino cheese to finish.

**SERVES 6-8
GUESTS AS
A STARTER**

RUBY COLESLAW

½ red cabbage, shredded
2 carrots, grated
1 red pepper, deseeded and finely sliced
1 yellow pepper, deseeded and finely sliced
1 onion, finely sliced
200g fresh peas (tinned as second best)

For the dressing
75ml peanut oil
50ml rice wine vinegar
2 tablespoons Lea & Perrins Worcestershire Sauce
1 tablespoon honey

1 Mix together all the vegetables in a large bowl – best to use your hands for this job.

2 In a separate bowl, whisk together all the dressing ingredients and then pour over the vegetables. Toss well so that everything is well coated. Cover and chill.

3 When ready to serve, bring back to room temperature. Great with barbecues, roast chicken and cold meats.

SERVES 6-8

FIRE!

Fire has threatened our beloved sauce twice. In 1882, on the 15th December, a fire began in the packing room at the Bank Street factory. Fortunately, it was discovered early and was extinguished. Damages were later valued at £17.11.6d. Then, in 1964, a large and very serious fire broke out in the Midland Road factory. Reports from the time confirm that twelve appliances and 50 men were needed to fight the fire. It required fourteen jets to quell the giant blaze. A huge amount of damage was caused, although, amazingly, full production was back underway just ten days later.

CREOLE PRAWNS WITH FETTUCCINE

25g unsalted butter
2 cloves garlic, minced
Handful basil leaves, torn
Small handful oregano leaves,
   roughly chopped
Good sprig of thyme, leaves
   only
$1/2$ teaspoon salt
Freshly ground black pepper
Level teaspoon cayenne
   pepper
3-4 plum tomatoes, skins
   removed after plunging into
   boiling water
150ml chicken stock
1 tablespoon Lea & Perrins
   Worcestershire Sauce
1 tablespoon hot chilli sauce
400g fettuccine
800g-1kg raw tiger prawns
   (according to budget!)

1 Melt the butter in a pan and add in the minced garlic, herbs, salt and peppers. Allow these to infuse over a gentle heat for a couple of minutes. Then add the tomatoes, stock, Worcestershire and chilli sauces and simmer gently for 10 minutes until you have a rich, fiery sauce.

2 Place the fettuccine in plenty of boiling salted water and cook for 10-12 minutes until the pasta is tender but still firm. Drain the pasta and return it to the pan to keep warm.

3 Add the prawns to the tomato sauce, turn up the heat and cook for 3-5 minutes or until the prawns have turned pink. Pour the sauce over the cooked fettuccine, toss the whole lot together and then serve on hot plates with plenty of ice-cold beer.

SERVES 4

Right
Add a little dash to your cooking....

Malt Vinegar

Molasses

Spirit Vinegar

Garlic

Anchovies

Shallots

Sugar

Tamarinds

Salt

Spices

IT TAKES US THREE YEARS TO
—— TURN THEM INTO ——
A BOTTLE OF LEA & PERRINS.

It only took Mr Lea and Mr Perrins a few days to make the first batch of Worcestershire Sauce in 1835. They prepared it for Lord Sandys, who'd discovered the recipe when he was governor of Bengal.

Everything went fine until the tasting. The sauce turned out to be throat-grippingly foul. Even Lord Sandys, who'd swallowed many a raging Vindaloo in Bengal, turned a ghastly shade of green.

With apologetic shrugs and a large dose of bicarbonate of soda for the queasy ex-governor, the sauce was consigned to the cellar in stone jars and quickly forgotten.

There was no time to dwell on failures. Lea & Perrins Chemist Shop was doing a roaring trade in everything from Taraxacum (dandelion coffee), to Dr Locock's Lotion For The Hair.

Some years later, during a general clearout, they came across the stone jars again. Scientific curiosity forced the two chemists to sample the contents once more.

They stared at each other in astonishment. The sauce tasted superb. It had matured.

They had stumbled across the vital missing ingredient: time.

What could be better for business than naming the sauce after their home town? The only question was what on earth you used it on. The answer was simple: everything.

People used it to enrich lamb hot-pots, steak and kidney pies, casseroles, fish, salads.

Others went further with dishes like Veal en Croûte, and Mushrooms à la Grecque.

By the time the Chinese got hold of it the list was as long as the Great Wall itself. (For a few suggestions try the L&P Cookbook advertised on our bottles.)

People are still finding new ways to use Lea & Perrins.

For instance, brushing it on white meat before microwaving improves both flavour and appearance. Talking of microwaves, surely we could devise a quicker way to make our sauce?

Perhaps we could. But even after 152 years, we can't quite forget the effect on Lord Sandys of our first attempt at high speed production.

DESKFAST PIZZA

1 ready-made pizza base
2 tablespoons tomato purée mixed with
1 teaspoon Lea & Perrins Worcestershire Sauce
2 pork and herb sausages cooked and thinly sliced
2 tomatoes, roughly chopped
2 sliced mushrooms
4 rashers of streaky bacon, grilled and diced
Drizzle of olive oil
1 handful rocket leaves

1 Pre-heat the oven to 200C/400F/Gas 6.

2 Take the pizza base and spread it with the tomato and Worcestershire sauce mixture. Place the sliced sausages over the pizza and top with the tomatoes and sliced mushrooms. Finally sprinkle the whole pizza with diced streaky bacon and drizzle with olive oil.

3 Pop the pizza onto a baking tray and into the hot oven for about 10-15 minutes or until the bacon is crispy. Cut into sections and top each wedge with a handful of rocket leaves.

4 Wrap up and take it to work for the perfect breakfast on the go or sneak it into the kids' lunchbox and they'll love you all day!

SERVES 2-4

Right
A turn-of-the-century triptych of reasons to trust Lea & Perrins.

LEA & PERRINS' SAUCE

The Original and Genuine Worcestershire

LEA & PERRINS' SAUCE

WAS INTRODUCED **OVER SIXTY YEARS AGO** AND NEVER VARIES IN EXCELLENCE OF QUALITY.

LEA & PERRINS' SAUCE

MANUFACTORY, WORCESTER, ENGLAND.

THE SIGNATURE IN WHITE ACROSS THE RED LABEL DISTINGUISHES THE ORIGINAL AND GENUINE WORCESTERSHIRE SAUCE.

LEA & PERRINS' SAUCE

IS MADE ONLY FROM THE **CHOICEST INGREDIENTS** AND KEEPS PERFECTLY IN EVERY CLIMATE.

SEARED BEEF SALAD WITH DATES & PISTACHIOS

400g rump steak
2 tablespoons Lea & Perrins
  Worcestershire Sauce
1 tablespoon olive oil
3 tablespoons walnut oil
1 tablespoon white wine
  vinegar
Salt and freshly ground black
  pepper
Handful flatleaf parsley
  leaves, roughly chopped
100g dates, stoned and sliced
40g shelled pistachio nuts
25g dried cranberries
Mixed salad leaves

1 Place the rump steak in a shallow dish and spoon over the Worcestershire sauce. Leave to marinate for at least an hour, turning the steak occasionally.

2 Heat the olive oil in a heavy based frying pan until just smoking. Remove the steak from the marinade and pat dry. Carefully put the steak into the hot oil and sear the beef for 2 minutes on each side so that it is crusty brown on the outside and rare on the inside. Take out the steak and leave to one side.

3 Whisk together the walnut oil and vinegar in a bowl and season with salt and pepper. In a separate bowl mix together the parsley leaves, dates, pistachios and cranberries then add the steak cut into thin slices.

4 Dress the salad leaves with the vinaigrette and scatter on 2 plates. Pile the steak mixture on top and season well with freshly milled black pepper. Serve with warm flatbreads or naan bread.

SERVES 2

RED LENTIL, TOMATO & STILTON SOUP

25g unsalted butter
1 medium onion, finely
   chopped
100g red lentils, washed
400g tin tomatoes
500ml semi-skimmed milk
250ml chicken stock
2 teaspoons Lea & Perrins
   Worcestershire Sauce
150g Stilton
Salt and freshly ground black
   pepper

1 Melt the butter in a heavy based saucepan and sauté the onion until soft. Add the red lentils and stir for a few minutes.

2 Add the tomatoes, milk, stock and Worcestershire sauce and keep stirring until it comes to the boil. Turn down the heat and simmer for 45 minutes, stirring occasionally.

3 Remove from the heat and crumble in the Stilton, stirring gently to melt it. Taste and season with salt and pepper as required. Serve with crusty French bread.

SERVES 4

RIDLEY CULE PROMOTIONS

PLEA & PORRIDGE SAUCE

FROM MR. OLIVER T. WIST'S
ORIGINAL MOOREISH RECIPE.

THE TWO-STEP SAUCE FOR ALL
WHO REQUIRE THAT LITTLE BIT MORE
FOR THEIR SUPPER.

IDEAL WITH GRUEL
AND OTHER MEAL DISHES.

AUDACIOUS IMPOSTERS!

GASCONY LAMB SHANKS

2 tablespoons olive oil
2 lamb shanks
1 onion, sliced
1 carrot, sliced
1 small leek, sliced
1 tablespoon flour
1 tablespoon tomato purée
1 tablespoon Lea & Perrins
  Worcestershire Sauce
2 glasses red wine
4 cloves garlic, peeled
8 cherry tomatoes, halved
1 tablespoon dried mixed
  herbs

1 Pre-heat the oven to 160C/325F/Gas 3.

2 Heat the oil in a heavy based casserole and brown the lamb shanks all over and then remove them from the pan. Pour out all but a little of the fat from the pan, add the onion, carrot and leek and cook them for a few minutes until softened.

3 Stir in the flour, tomato purée, Worcestershire sauce and cook for a couple of minutes. Add in the wine, bring to the boil and then simmer for 10 minutes. Add the remaining ingredients and put back the lamb shanks together with enough water to just cover the meat.

4 Replace the casserole lid and cook in the oven for 2-3 hours. Check and stir the casserole from time to time and add a little more water if it looks too dry. The sauce should be thick and rich and the meat should just fall away from the bone.

SERVES 2

Right Fit for a monarch's table. King Edward VII granted the rare Royal Warrant to Lea & Perrins in 1904.

GLOBE ARTICHOKES WITH SESAME TARRAGON DIP

4 globe artichokes
Juice of 1 lemon
1 teaspoon salt

For the dip
200ml mayonnaise
2 tablespoons Lea & Perrins
  Worcestershire Sauce
1 tablespoon olive oil
1 tablespoon sesame oil
1 tablespoon runny honey
1 tablespoon lemon juice
1 teaspoon finely chopped
  tarragon
Sea salt and freshly ground
  black pepper

1 Prepare the dip in advance by whisking together all the dipping ingredients. Cover and refrigerate.

2 Cut the artichoke stems down to the base of the globe so that they will stand up. Put the 4 globes side by side in a large pan and add water until it comes two thirds of the way up the artichokes. Add the lemon juice and salt and bring to the boil. Reduce to a simmer, cover and leave cooking for 30-35 minutes.

3 After this time lift out one of the artichokes with a slotted spoon. When cooked the bottom 'petals' should fall away from the globe. Drain and serve on a large plate with a small bowl of dipping sauce each.

4 To eat, simply pull off each petal, dip in the sauce and bite off the fleshy base, discarding the rest of the petal. When you reach the centre of the artichoke, remove the hairy leaves on the top and eat the heart - it's the best of all!

SERVES 4

SSHHH! DON'T SPILL THE SECRET

In 1911, the secret ingredient was nearly revealed when one of the new partners died, and his papers and documents were being decided over. The directors of Lea & Perrins, fearfully realising that a copy of the recipe might be found, swiftly gave instructions to seal the envelope containing the information. The secret has remained safe ever since .

CUMBERLAND VENISON STEAKS

For the sauce
2 tablespoons cranberry
   sauce
Zest and juice of $1/2$ lime
Zest and juice of $1/2$ orange
2 teaspoons Lea & Perrins
   Worcestershire Sauce
$1/2$ teaspoon grated ginger
$1/2$ teaspoon mustard powder
100ml port

2 venison steaks
1 teaspoon crushed mixed
   peppercorns
1 tablespoon vegetable oil
1 large shallot, finely chopped

1 You can make the sauce in advance to make life easier. Put the cranberry sauce, fruit juice and zest, Worcestershire sauce, ginger and mustard powder into a pan and bring up to a simmer whisking to combine all the ingredients. Remove from the heat, stir in the port and keep until ready to use.

2 Pat the venison steaks dry with some kitchen paper and then press in the crushed peppercorns on both sides of the steaks. Heat the oil in a heavy based pan until smoking and then add the venison. The steaks will need to cook for 4-5 minutes each side for medium. You can reduce or increase the time for rare or well done by 1 minute. Halfway through cooking, add the shallots to the pan tucking them in around the steaks and not on top.

3 Just before the steaks are cooked to your liking add the sauce and let it bubble in the hot pan for 30 seconds. Serve the steaks with the shallots and sauce poured over accompanied by crispy jacket potatoes and a good leafy salad.

SERVES 2

L&P LIPTAUER CHEESE

250g cream cheese
1 tablespoon capers, rinsed
and drained
1 tablespoon Lea & Perrins
Worcestershire Sauce
1 tablespoon mild mustard
1 tablespoon sweet smoked
paprika
Salt and freshly ground black
pepper

1 Mash the cream cheese in a bowl. Pound the capers into a paste and mix them into the cheese. Stir in the Worcestershire sauce, mustard and paprika. Blend the whole mixture well. Taste and add salt and pepper if required.

2 Serve with sliced dill pickles and good dark rye bread.

SERVES 4-6

CORNED BEEF HASH

200g corned beef
2 tablespoons Lea & Perrins
   Worcestershire sauce
1 teaspoon whole grain
   mustard
1 large onion
275g potatoes (Desirée or
   King Edward)
2-3 tablespoons olive oil
Salt and freshly ground black
   pepper
2 large free-range eggs

1 Dice the corned beef into 1cm cubes and scoop into a bowl. Mix together the Worcestershire sauce and mustard in a cup, pour over the corned beef and mix well. Peel and halve the onion, cut into half moons. Scrub, but do not peel the potatoes and cut into 1cm cubes.

2 Place the potatoes in a saucepan and pour enough boiling water from the kettle to almost cover them, add salt, a lid and simmer for 5 minutes. Drain in a colander and leave aside.

3 Heat the oil in a large heavy based frying pan until smoking hot, add the onions and toss in the oil for three minutes until well browned. Add the potatoes and toss until browned then season with a little salt and a good grind of pepper. Finally add the corned beef mixture and continue to toss everything in the pan for about three minutes.

4 In a separate pan fry the eggs. Serve the hash divided onto two warm plates with a fried egg on top of each.

SERVES 2

STICKY HONEY RIBS

For the marinade
4 tablespoons white wine vinegar
2 tablespoons soy sauce
2 tablespoons Lea & Perrins Worcestershire Sauce
2 red chillies, deseeded and chopped
1 teaspoon chopped fresh ginger
1/2 teaspoon ground cinnamon
1 tablespoon sesame oil
1 tablespoon groundnut oil

16 good meaty pork spare ribs
2 tablespoons runny honey
2 spring onions, chopped
Small bunch coriander, chopped

1 Mix together all the marinade ingredients in a jug. Put the ribs into a large, strong plastic bag and pour in the marinade. Seal or knot the bag and squidge the whole lot round so that all the ribs are coated with the gooey mixture. Leave in a cool place for a couple of hours or ideally in the fridge overnight.

2 Pre-heat the oven to 200C/400F/Gas 6. Empty the contents of the bag into a suitable roasting tin, cover with foil and pop into the oven for 1 hour.

3 Remove the foil and drizzle the runny honey over the ribs. Put them back in the oven, uncovered for a further 20-25 minutes, turning once during this time.

4 Pile the ribs onto a warmed serving plate and scatter with spring onions and coriander.

SERVES 4

BOTTLE IT

Most sauces in 1837 – the time when Lea and Perrins Worcestershire Sauce began to be commercially produced – were sold in square bottles. The origin of the round Lea & Perrins bottle lies in the fact that the sauce had originally been decanted into the standard trade medicine bottles that Lea & Perrins – who, let us not forget, were chemists – poured all of their mixtures. The design stuck!

LAMB CHOPS WITH WORCESTERSHIRE MINT SAUCE

2 red peppers, deseeded and
  quartered
2 tablespoons olive oil
Good pinch of sugar
Sea salt and freshly ground
  black pepper
1 aubergine, sliced
8 lamb chops

**Combine the following to
make the mint sauce**
2 tablespoons Lea & Perrins
  Worcestershire Sauce
Handful fresh mint leaves,
  finely chopped
Good pinch caster sugar

1 Pre-heat the oven to 200C/400F/Gas 6. Put the quartered peppers in a roasting dish and drizzle them with the olive oil. Sprinkle the sugar over them and then season with plenty of salt and pepper. Roast for 30 minutes.

2 While the peppers cook, cut the aubergine into 1cm slices, brush with olive oil and season. Heat a griddle pan or large non-stick frying pan over a fairly high heat and sear the slices in batches until golden on both sides. Put them aside on a plate.

3 In the same pan brown the chops on both sides. Take the roasting dish of cooked peppers and lay the aubergine slices on top. Next add the chops and put the whole lot back in the oven for 15-20 minutes.

4 To serve, divide the chops, peppers and aubergines between 4 warmed serving plates and spoon over the Worcestershire mint sauce.

My good friend Ken, without any vinegar to make his mint sauce one day, reached for the Lea & Perrins and created this brilliant variation. He's been making it this way ever since!

SERVES 4

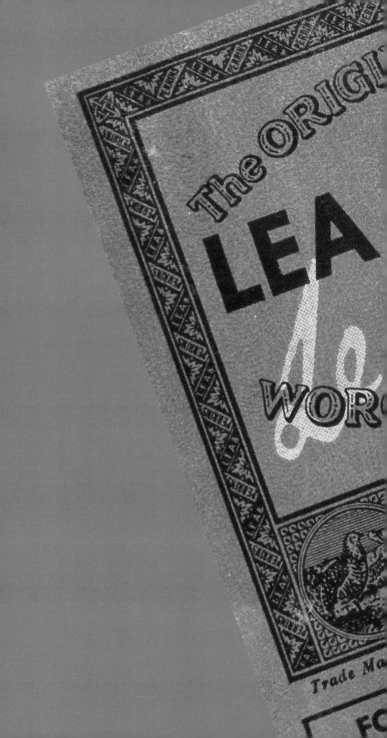

AL and GENUINE

PERRINS
SAUCE

ESTERSHIRE SAUCE

Lea Perrins

istered by LEA & PERRINS LTD.

Marca Registrada

SOUPS, STEWS, GRILLS, MEATS, GRAVIES,
CHEESE DISHES, and with TOMATO JUICE

CONTENTS 5 FL. OZ.

& PERRINS LTD., at their

ESTER, ENGLAND

A SPLASH OF HISTORY

1791

John Wheeley Lea was born. One of three sons and four daughters he was raised in a farming family. As a young man, he chose to become a chemist.

1793

William Henry Perrins was born. Oddly enough, he too was one of three sons and four daughters and was raised in a farming family. As a young man, he also chose to become a chemist.

1823

John Lea & William Perrins decided to go into partnership together. They prepared a catalogue ready for their commencement on 1st January 1823 at the Broad Street shop.

1825

Following from their success, Lea & Perrins opened a branch shop in Kidderminster. Managed by a Mr Court, the shop was named Lea, Perrins and Court.

1830-ish

Returning from Bengal to his Worcestershire home, the aristocrat Lord Sandys asked local chemists John Lea and William Perrins to make up a recipe for a sauce that he had picked up on his travels. Having carried out these instructions, it is thought that the pair of chemists kept aside a few samples of the sauce for themselves. Upon eventually trying it they found the taste to be quite disgusting, and stashed the jars of sauce at the back of the cellar. When they stumbled upon the jars a few years later, they planned to discard them, but thought they would try the mixture one last time before doing so. To their utter amazement, Lord Sandy's concoction had matured into something altogether different: a tantalising, mouthwatering sauce. The chemists set to bottling their creation and, in just a matter of years, it had become known and indispensable to cooks all over the world.

1837

Lea & Perrins Worcestershire Sauce began to be produced commercially.

Late 1830s

In a show of great business acumen, Lea & Perrins managed to get cases of their sauce onto all ocean liners that came in and out of British waters. A fee was paid to the on-board stewards, who served the sauce in the dining rooms. Passengers tried the sauce, and, intrigued, would then request to buy a bottle to take home. It didn't take long for word to get around, and Lea & Perrins' fame grew quickly.

1839

A New York entrepreneur by the name of John Duncan ordered a small quantity of Lea & Perrins Worcestershire Sauce. He liked the sauce a lot and saw its potential. In just a few years, Duncan had begun to import large shipments to keep up with demand Stateside. Lea & Perrins was the only commercially bottled condiment available and the Americans couldn't get enough of it. When importing the sauce at such volume became impractical, Duncan opened a processing plant, and imported the ingredients from England to make his own sauce using the same English formula.

It was luck, more than science, that led to chemists Lea & Perrins creating their amazing sauce.

1840

Another branch shop opened in Malvern, called Lea & Perrins & Burrows. An office and warehouse was also opened in London.

1867

William Henry Perrins died.

1874

John Wheeley Lea died.

1882

15 December. In the early hours of the morning, a fire began in the packing room at the Bank Street factory. Luckily, it was discovered early and extinguished.

1892

Charles (the son of John Wheeley) retired. This marked the ending of the Lea family's involvement with the sauce company.

1904

King Edward VII granted the Royal Warrant to Lea & Perrins. A rare and prestigious honour, Lea & Perrins would go on to hold this warrant up to the present day (the present one having been granted by Queen Elizabeth II).

1911

The secret ingredient was very nearly revealed when one of the new partners died. Luckily, Lea & Perrins were alert to the danger of the recipe being found and gave strict instructions that the envelope containing the information be sealed. The secret was safe once more.

1916

The Spanish Royal Warrant is granted to Lea & Perrins by the King of Spain.

1930

On June 11th, Lea & Perrins was sold to HP Foods.

1940

Activity at the Midland Road factory was suspended due to fear of an invasion in Worcester. The bottling plant was moved to the premises of HP Foods at Aston Cross, Birmingham, which ensured that production could be kept going.

1941

Production of Lea & Perrins Worcestershire Sauce continued throughout the war, but at a reduced scale. There was a shortage of manpower and there were difficulties in importing some of the ingredients. At the beginning of the year, a temporary label was issued when the regular label printing plant was hit by enemy fire.

1942

The War Department, implementing emergency powers, took possession of the Midland Road factory. The Royal Army Ordinance Corps took control of the vaults, using them as a depot for vehicle and tank parts.

Yet, despite this, a small area of the factory still continued to manufacture the sauce, with records showing 44 staff on the Lea & Perrins books at this time.

1943

Official documents show that staff numbers were now reduced to 25 working at the factory. There were also 25 people enlisted as volunteers, working as night watchmen among other things.

1945

Every single member of staff who left the factory after being called up for war services found that their jobs still awaited them on their return. Whilst sourcing ingredients remained very difficult, figures show that production levels were well on their way to returning to normal.

1964

A fire broke out in the Midland Road factory, of a much bigger magnitude than the one which damaged the Bank Street factory over 75 years previously. More than 50 men were required to fight the blaze. A huge amount of damage was caused, yet, miraculously, production levels returned to normal just ten days later.

1988

The French multi-national food company BSN (later re-named Danone) purchased HP Foods Ltd.

2002

Lea & Perrins launch their international web-site, www.leaperrins.com.

2005

Lea & Perrins is bought by US food company, Heinz.

AUTHOR'S ACKNOWLEDGMENTS

As with my previous two books, I have friends and colleagues to thank for their help and contributions. Firstly, my wife Lynda, who like me cannot imagine a store cupboard without Lea & Perrins Worcestershire Sauce, and who has listened patiently to my every new and enthusiastic recipe idea, helped me create it and, of course, tasted it. A big thank you goes to Sarah Francis, our friend and tutor at Whatley Grange Cookery School in Somerset who carefully checks the recipes, fine-tunes the techniques and adds her own invaluable tips. My grateful thanks go to our friends and customers at Hartley's FGF who always come up with ideas, recipes and inspiration to make our books special, namely Ken, Betty and Jerry, Chrissie, Sarah and Ross – well done guys! Last, but by no means least, thank you to the team at Absolute Press – Jon Croft (the boss), Meg Avent and Matt Inwood. As ever, they have really come up with the goodies and have made The Lea & Perrins Worcestershire Sauce Cookbook the third in a series of great iconic food books.

PICTURE CREDITS

All pictures courtesy of Lea & Perrins, except for p17, p25, p35, p37, p47, p49, p55, p65, p72 all © Robert Opie Picture Collection; and p14 © Intergloria / The Kobal Collection; p27 © Svensk Flilmindustri / The Kobal Collection; p32 © ABC/Cinerama / The Kobal Collection; p38 © Universal / The Kobal Collection; p50 © Paramount / The Kobal Collection; p57 © 20the Century Fox / The Kobal Collection; p77 © Universal / The Kobal Collection. The publishers would like to thank Lea & Perrins, especially Roma Phulwani and Paul Harvey. Thanks also to Robert Opie and to Caroline and Darren at the Kobal Collection.